GABRIEL PIERNÉ

THE CHILDREN AT BETHLEHEM

A MYSTERY IN TWO PARTS
POEM BY GABRIEL NIGOND

. .

ENGLISH TRANSLATION BY
M. LOUISE BAUM

CHILDREN'S CHORUS PARTS CONDENSED

NEW YORK : G. SCHIRMER

The Children at Bethlehem
Children's Chorus Parts
Part I
The Plain

The pasture-lands surrounding a village. In the winter twilight a group of shepherd-children are watching their flocks

Gabriel Pierné

The Narrater
But braving the cold, tho' it bite so sore, And loath to leave the year's last pasture-land,

Blithe of heart, a frolicsome band, The shepherd children dance once more.

The Children (gaily)

Heads of brown and heads of

yel-low, Red-head makes a brav-er show, Red-head makes a brav-er

4

lies. _____

⑦ **Children** _mf_
Jack and Joan they cried for the moon, sir! How she mocked them from the

a tempo
_mf_

blue! Jack and Joan (my tale's be - gun, sir!) One, sir! Thought they'd best be

⑧ **(almost shouted)**
laughing, too! Two! One, sir! Two! Pot of oil and pot of hon-ey, Love is

nev - er bought for mon - ey, Love is free to you and me! Three!

6

say, "O Maid - en Ma - ry, Who toil-est in field and dair - y, Thou hast

found the King's own son!" One! "Thou hast found the King's own son!"

Now we're done! Now we are done, five, six, sev - en! All good

chil-dren go to heav'n! One, two, three, four, five, six, sev-en! All good children go to

8

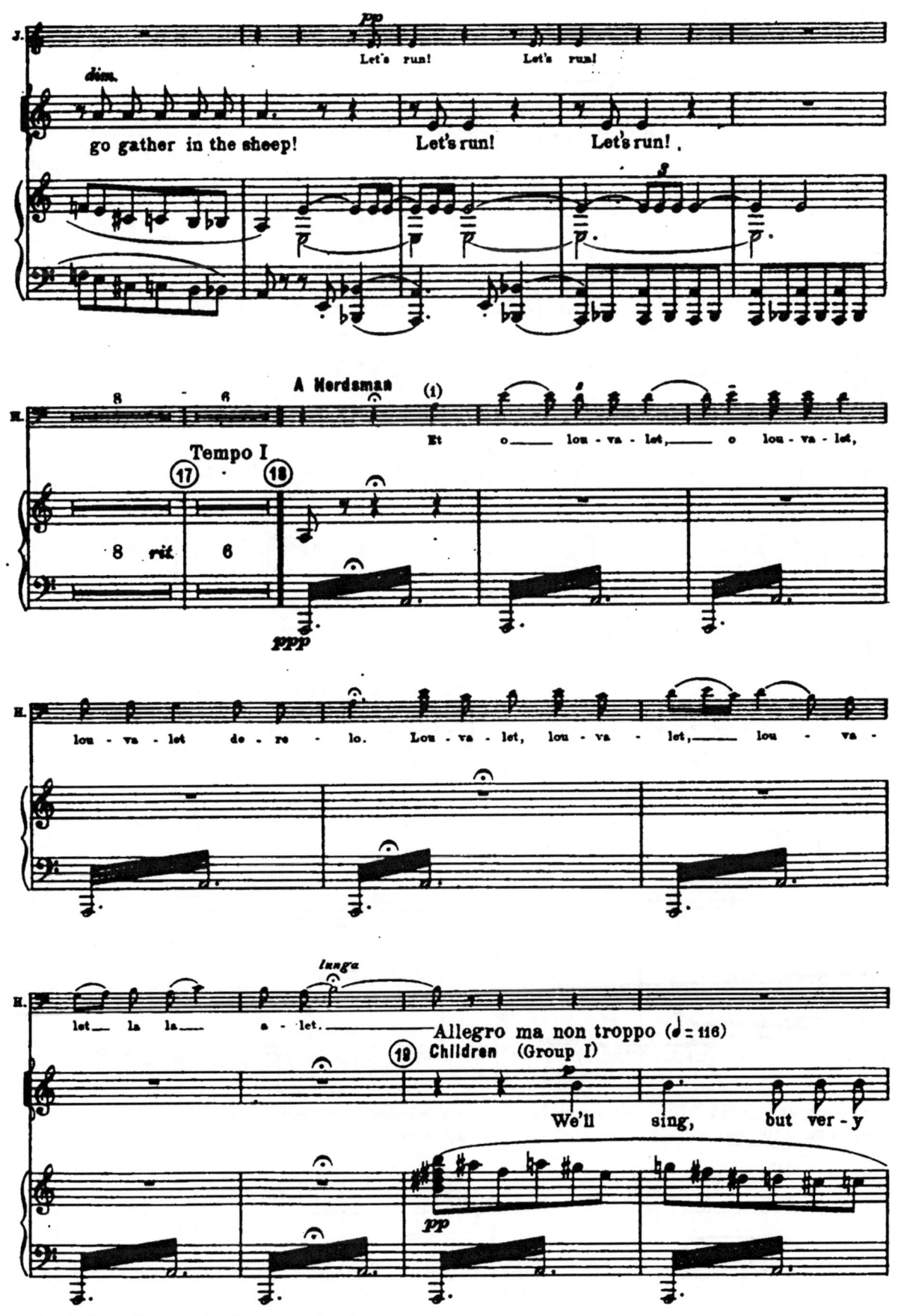

(1) Call of the shepherds to their sheep

(Group II) *p*

low! We'll sing, but ver-y low! Hand in hand let us

poco

poco

(All) *poco*

go! Hand in hand let us go!_____

(Group I)

We'll sing, but ver-y low! So the

(Group II)

pp

⑳ **(All)**

naughty sprite can-not find us, And with ne'er a glance be - hind us, On our

(They start off. They hurry, but do not go

homeward way we go! *cresc.*

very fast, and as the little ones are ready to cry, the older ones begin to sing, in weak voices, trembling with fear, an old lament of the chimney corner.)

f

dim.

poco rit.

The Children

㉑ (Group I)

p dolente

In my father's field Chanti-cleers are three,

(Group II) *p*

In my father's field

a tempo

leggero

Chanticleers are three;

(All)

One. asleep with drooping wings,

One his nois-y challenge flings,

One that neither sleeps nor sings, one that

㉒ *doloroso* *rinf.* *dim.*

neither sleeps nor sings! Ah! la, la, la, la, la, la, la, la, la!

rinf. *dim.*

(Group I) *rit* *p a tempo*

In my father's fold Three white lambs there be,

(Group II) *p*

In my father's fold

rit *p a tempo*

(All)

Three white lambs there be;____ One to crop the tender grass,

One to chase the winds that pass,____ One to love and fol-low me, one to

(23) *doloroso rinf.* *dim.*

love and fol-low me!____ Ah! la, la, la,____ la, la, la,____ la, la, la!

rit *a tempo* *dim. sempre*

In my fa-ther's fold Three white lambs there be,____

THE STAR

No - ël!____ No - ël! No-

molto PP **(24)** *a tempo*

In my fa-ther's fold Three white lambs there be.____

PP

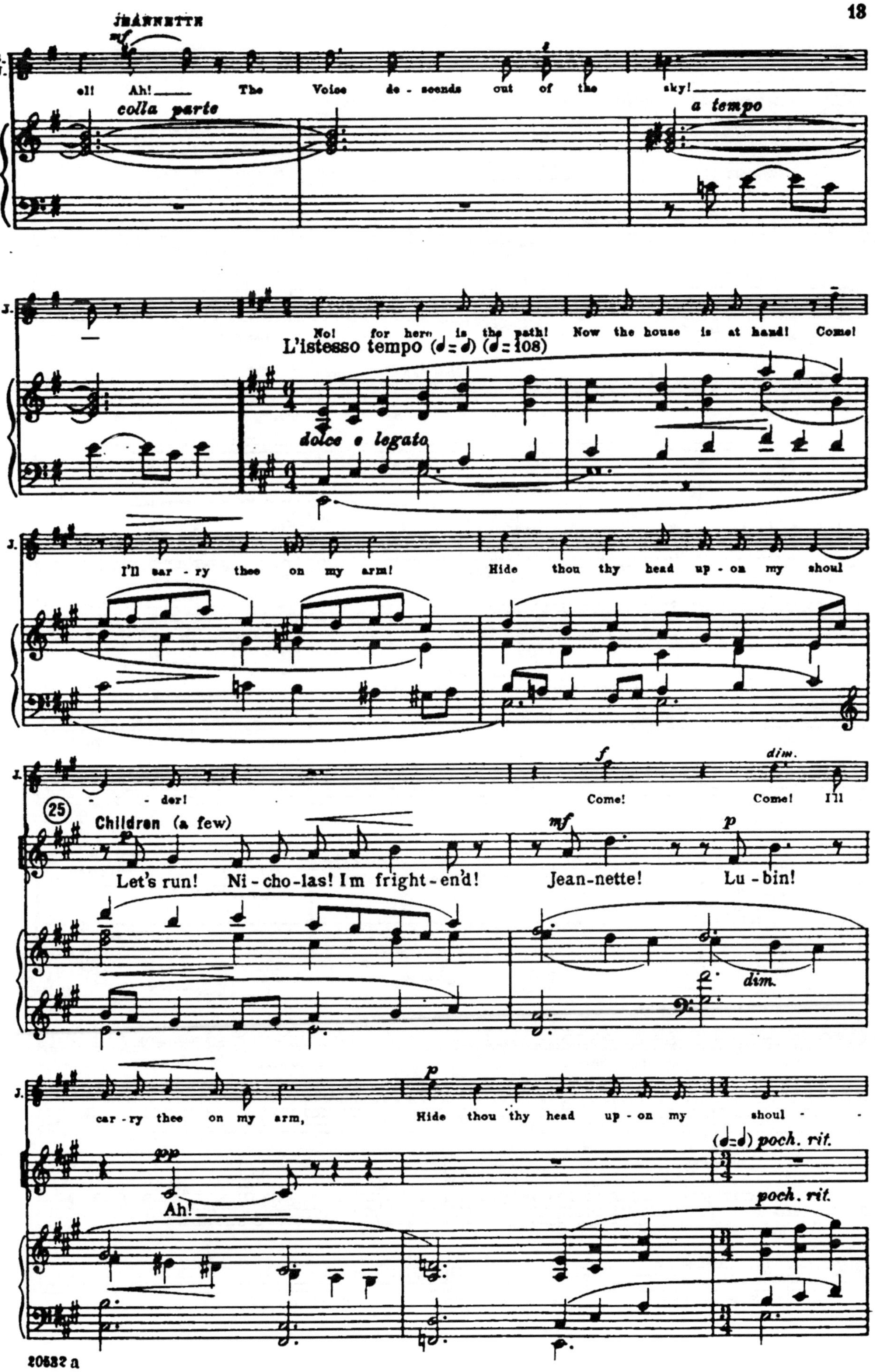
JEANNETTE
mf
S.
J.
e! Ah! The Voice de-scends out of the sky!
colla parte
a tempo
No! for here is the path! Now the house is at hand! Come!
L'istesso tempo (♩=♩) (♩=108)
dolce e legato
I'll car-ry thee on my arm! Hide thou thy head up-on my shoul-der!
25
f
dim.
Come! Come! I'll
Children (a few)
mf
p
Let's run! Ni-cho-las! I'm fright-en'd! Jean-nette! Lu-bin!
dim.
p
car-ry thee on my arm, Hide thou thy head up-on my shoul-
pp
Ah!
(♩=♩) poch. rit.
poch. rit.

14

20582 a

15

18

L.

hap- -py!   am   hap-   -py,   And   yet   am   I

In   my   fa - ther's fold   Three white lambs there be,   In   my   fa - ther's fold

(33)

L.

fain   to   weep! _____   Ah!   be   it

Group I

We   brave the cold   and the north-wind,   Be it

Group II

Three   white lambs there be.   We   brave the cold   and the north-wind,   Be it

L.
S.

blow- -ing   low   or   high! _____   Be - hold!   now   the   Sav-   -iour

THE STAR (slowly and with majesty)

blow - ing   low   or   high! _____

Un poco allarg. (ma poco)

(34)

20532 a

20

20582 a

The lit - tle Christ-Child suf - fers so!

NICHOLAS

Nich - o - las, bring thy warm, new man - - tle! Sin - ter,

JEANNETTE

no! No! 'Tis not worth the trou - - ble. The babe has

naught to keep Him warm.

Children (a few)

The babe has naught to keep Him warm.

one hump! Look! look at the fourth, he has two! Hi!

NICHOLAS

See!

bears! How fierce their little eyes are! Do not let them come too near to you!

See! Be-neath his tin-sel trap - -ings, Pur-ple, or - ange, red. blue and

yel - -low. See, he comes! The el - e - phant comes!

Who-ev-er may de - ny Thee, To Thee I take my way!

Who-ev-er may de - ny Thee, To Thee I take my way!

THE STAR

No - ël! No - ël! No - ël!

con entusiasmo

un poco allargando (♩=76)

We brave the cold and the north-wind,

No - ël! No - ël! No - ël!

Let him blow low_ or high!

Part II

The Stable

34

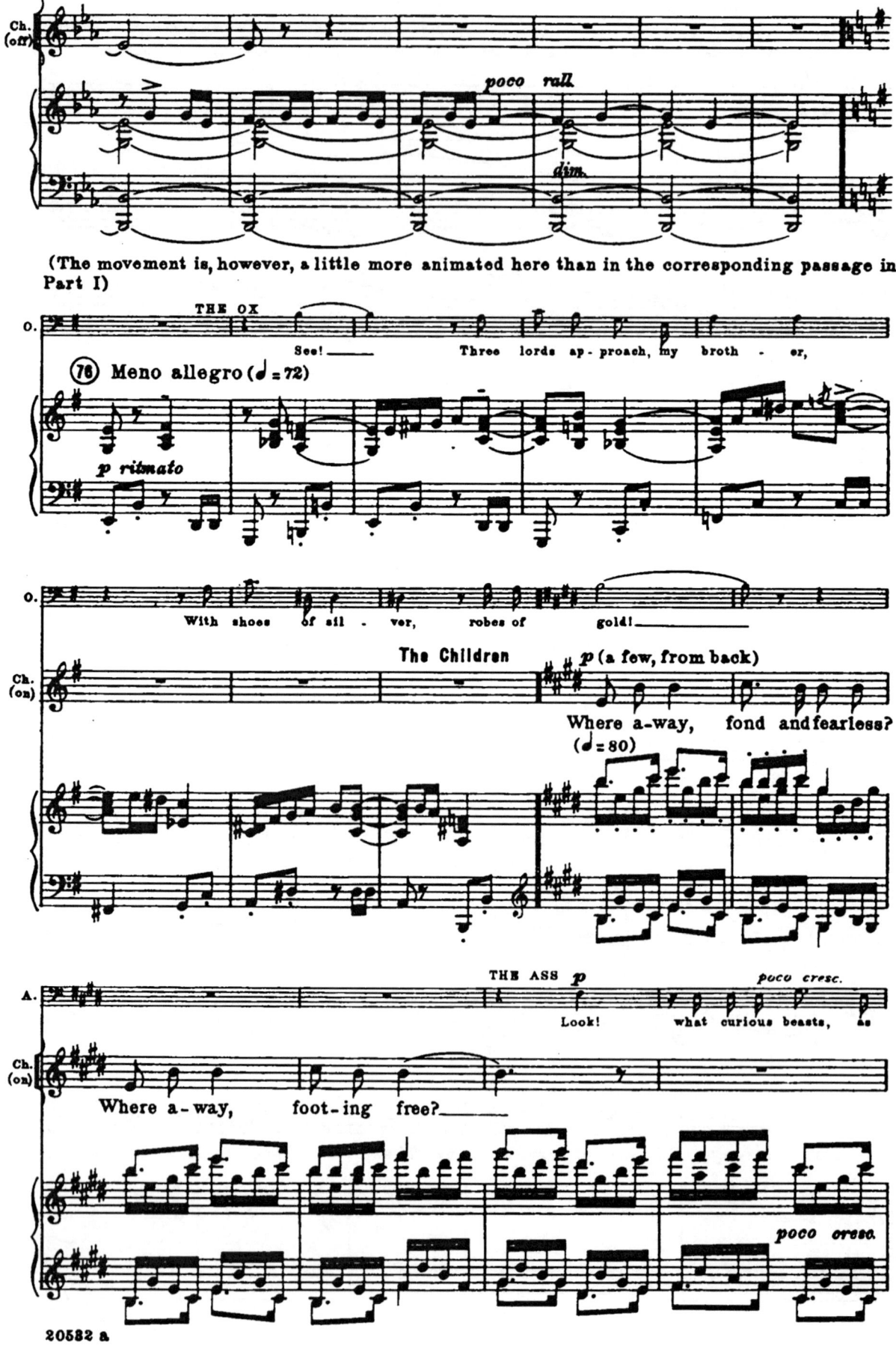

(The movement is, however, a little more animated here than in the corresponding passage in Part I)

THE OX

See!_____ Three lords ap-proach, my broth - er,

(76) Meno allegro (♩=72)

p ritmato

With shoes of sil - ver, robes of gold!_____

The Children

p (a few, from back)

Where a-way, fond and fearless?
(♩=80)

THE ASS p

poco cresc.

Look! what curious beasts, as

Where a-way, foot-ing free?_____

poco cresc.

20532 a

38

20582 a

44

46

♪=♪; beat the eighth-notes)

(They present their humble gifts)   *dolce*

Dear Sav-iour Je-sus, re-ceive us,

Children   *dolce*

Dear Sav-iour Je-sus, re-ceive us,

dolce

Dear Sav-iour Je-sus, re-ceive us,

a tempo

sosten.   (accomp. ad lib.) *)

Chil-dren who tend flocks and herds;   We've brought Thee

Chil-dren who tend flocks and herds;   We've brought Thee

Chil-dren who tend flocks and herds;   We've brought Thee

(ad lib.)

milk and some ap-ples,   New white bread and cream-y curds.

milk and some ap-ples,   New white bread and cream-y curds.

milk and some ap-ples,   New white bread and cream-y curds.

p

*)This passage in 3 parts may be sung as a unison on the first part, in which case the ac-
companiment is necessary

°0582 a

Who with balm-y breath so mild Have comfort-ed His dis - tress - es!

Who with balm-y breath so mild Have comfort-ed His dis - tress - es!

Who with balm-y breath so mild Have comfort-ed His dis - tress - es!

THE ASS

Ye young things, your kind so - li - ci -

ta - tions To ten - der - ness move a rude heart!

For lov - ing word and ca - ress Fall rare - ly e - nough to our part.

50

THE STAR

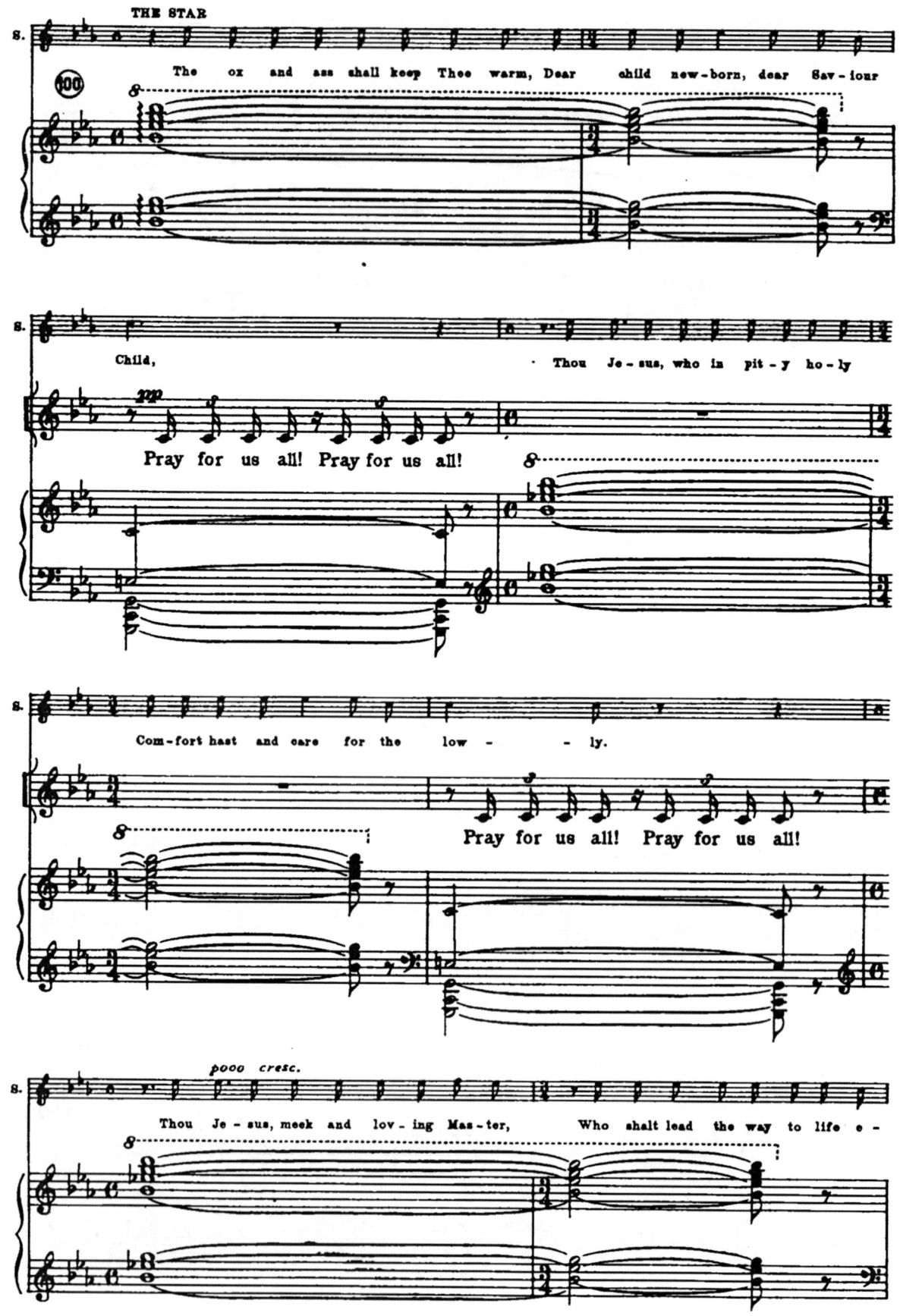

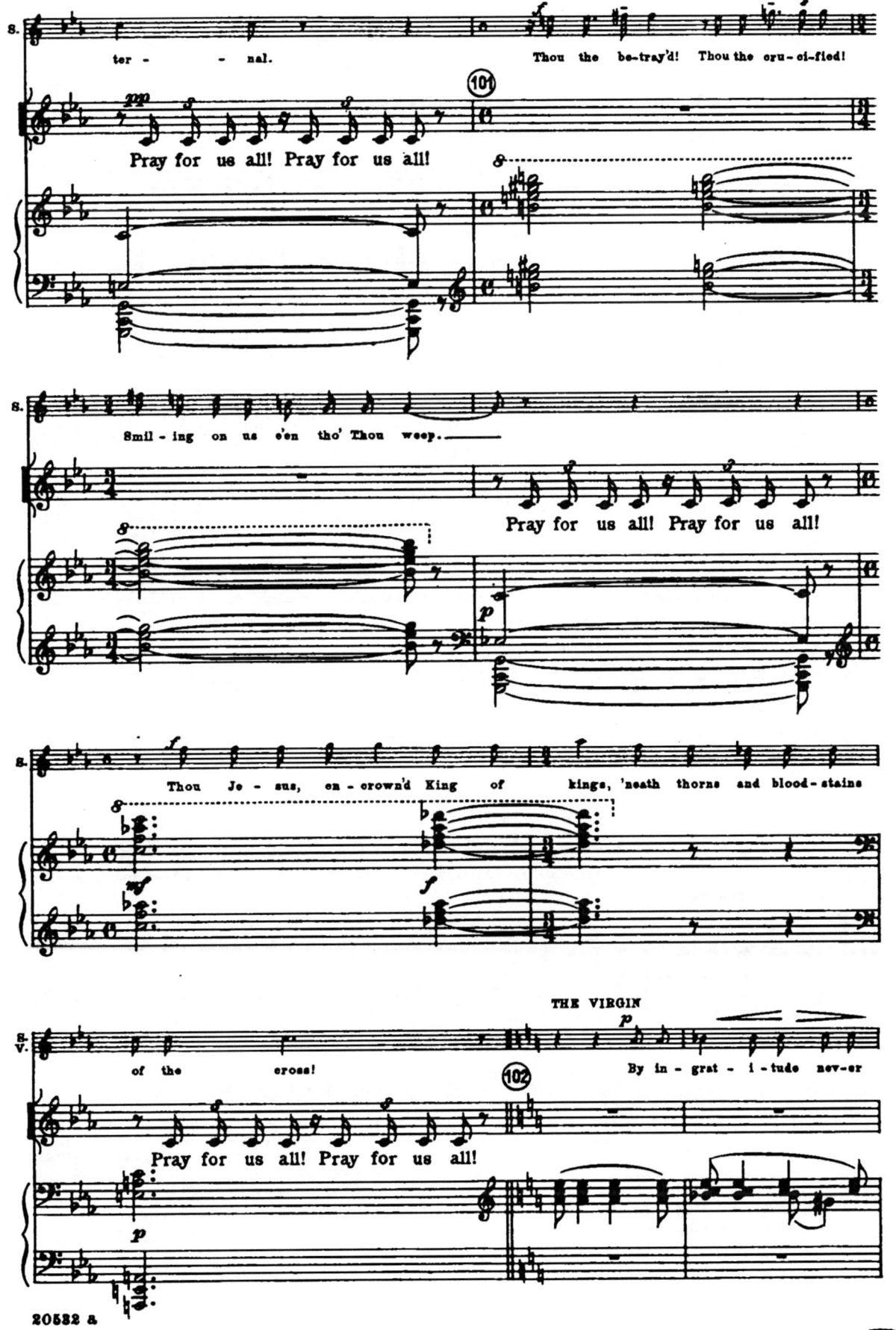

V.
fend - - er! Then pray for Him in heav - en's
We'll pray for Him!
V.
name, And in the name of His moth - - er!
pp
We'll pray for Him!
(on)
(off)
p (off stage)
We'll pray for Him!

(The Virgin is again alone beside the manger, over which the Ox and the Ass have continued to breathe)

Lightning Source UK Ltd.
Milton Keynes UK
04 October 2010

160760UK00002B/2/A